Wonderfully *Made*

Women, Faith, and Self-Care

Terri J. Plank Brenneman

Harrisonburg, Virginia
Waterloo, Ontario

Wonderfully Made
Women, Faith, and Self-Care

Hymns referenced in this book are from *Hymnal: A Worship Book* (Faith & Life Resources, 1992), *Sing the Journey* (Faith & Life Resources, 2005), and *Sing the Story* (Faith & Life Resources, 2007).

The content for this book was sponsored jointly by Mennonite Women USA and Mennonite Women Canada.

International Standard Book Number: 978-0-8361-9574-3.
Design by Merrill Miller, Mary Meyer
Cover photo: Soren Pilman/iStockphoto/Thinkstock
Printed in the USA

16 15 14 13 12 11 10   10 9 8 7 6 5 4 3 2 1

To order or request information, please call 1-800-245-7894 in the U.S. or 1-800-631-6535 in Canada.

www.mpn.net

Contents

Preface

Treated to a favorite menu—tea and scones—I was approached by a dear colleague to consider writing this Bible study guide on the topic of self-care. She primed the pump well with her sumptuous fare! One of my most pleasurable acts of self-care is to have afternoon tea at a lovely antique store tea room nearby.

Writing about self-care resonated with me from the start. I know the concept well from my training as a clinical psychologist. My work with Mennonite Women in the United States and Canada gave me a deep appreciation for the gifts women bring to the world. I know the benefits of caring for ourselves to sustain our creative endeavors and to carry out our many caregiving tasks. To offer good and healthy care to others, we need to nurture and replenish ourselves, our primary resource. My seminary training in biblical studies added another reason to write this guide. I seemed to have all the right tools.

The challenge in writing the guide was that, well, it is a Bible study guide, after all. Where to find the biblical support for what I know to be true? Especially since so much of my early learning can be summed up in the old Sunday school song about "Jesus first, others next, yourself last." I did not want to search for Scriptures to support a concept. I wanted to let the Scriptures call us to the need for and benefit of self-care.

Developing my first outline, I entitled it "Everything I need to know about self-care I learned through infertility." For it was through this challenging life circumstance that I came face to face with my personal and spiritual limitations. I had to learn new ways of caring for myself: body, mind, and spirit. This devastating experience ultimately resulted in a deeper self- and spiritual transformation than I could ever have imagined. That transformation came through acts of self-care where I met God through Scripture, prayer, and meditation.

As I wrote these sessions, I rediscovered the spiritual practice of self-care. At least, that is what these lessons became for me. May they enrich your personal and spiritual life as they have mine.

Terri J. Plank Brenneman
Goshen, Indiana

A Word on the Use of This Guide

Spiritual growth involves learning to know God through the Scriptures and through life experience. Thus the sessions in this guide begin with a scriptural overview and move to personal experience through the visuals and thoughts of the gathering time. The "Deepening" part of each session returns to reflection on Scripture, and is followed by "Integrating" questions that relate the lesson to our own lives. The "Closing" section brings together both scriptural insights and life-lessons in an atmosphere of prayer.

Women can use this guide in a variety of ways.

1. Both individual reflection and/or group sharing. Women read the lessons during the week, or at the beginning of the session, and choose one or two questions to ponder. In the group setting, each participant might then share her thoughts and insights with the others. This approach recognizes that group sharing is deeply enriched through time for personal reflection. The role of the leader is to facilitate sharing rather than to "teach" the lessons. The leader will need to focus on one or two questions rather than trying to include them all.

2. An individual or informal study. An individual can study the Bible text and meditate on the words, perhaps using a journal to make entries and notice how God is walking with her. Or a group of friends may sit around the kitchen table and study the lessons together.

3. A more traditional approach. For a more formal Bible study, the makeup of your group is essential to the style you choose as leader. A teaching group is more likely to emphasize the "Deepening" section rather than the integrating questions, which are quite personal in nature. Here are a few questions the leader might use to promote interaction with the material presented in the "Deepening" section:

- How have you understood this passage in the past?
- What is new or different about the ideas presented here?
- What do you find interesting or intriguing?
- What makes you uncomfortable?
- What feelings do you notice as you reflect on this lesson?
- How might the Spirit be inviting you to grow?

4. Shorter meditations. The group or individual might want to use only the overview, visuals, and gathering for shorter meditations. A more elderly group, for example, may not be inclined to ask the deeper, probing questions. They might be very responsive, however, to sharing stories and memories sparked by the section on gathering.

Whatever the makeup of your group, pray for spiritual growth in an atmosphere of trust, confidentiality, and respect. As women of faith, may we grow in confidence and wisdom as we receive our gifts from God and share them with others.

one . . . .

Self-Care: Breathe

READING: Ezekiel 37:4-5, 9

OVERVIEW

God takes the prophet Ezekiel to a valley where dry, wasted bones are scattered across the land. Then God poses the question, "Can these bones live?" Ezekiel responds with the experience of one who has previously faced God's conundrums. "O Lord God, you know." As the text relates, the life breath, the spirit of God breathes into the dry, lifeless bones, solving the puzzle. New living beings can come out of death and emptiness. This vision provides hope for the exiled people of Israel who feel lost, dried up and discouraged. God promises, "I will put my spirit within you, and you shall live."

VISUAL: Picture of desert scene or sand tray; items that symbolize dryness

GATHERING

As I prepared to lead a retreat for Mennonite Women in Southern California, my wise husband-pastor nudged me to use my struggle with infertility as the basis for my speaking. I chose the theme of barrenness for the retreat. A challenge, to be sure.

As I reviewed images of barrenness in the biblical accounts, the desert landscape of my surroundings surfaced. Dry, empty stretches of sand for miles on end. A desolation so complete it seemed nothing could survive this habitat. It reminded me of what Ezekiel saw as he surveyed the Valley of Dry Bones: death, destruction, and the improbability of life ever reviving the scorched, disconnected bones.

The image mirrored my internal landscape—my barren womb littered with unconceived children, my soul with empty hopes and dreams. Endless days, months, years of dying little by little. How could new life revive these dry bones?

Focusing on my breath going in and out, I began to identify the shattered and broken parts of my life.

Just breathe! A breath awareness exercise unlocked the mystery for me. Focusing on my breath going in and out, I began to identify the shattered and broken parts of my life. Experiencing God's breath coming from the "four winds," picking up those pieces and re-fashioning my hopes and expectations, gave me life anew.

One of my therapy clients in her hard-won wisdom said, "God, does not make new things; God makes things new." And so God took my battered ideals and wishes and reshaped them into gifts far greater than I could have imagined. God-breathed spirit made my life new.

DEEPENING

In both the Old and New Testaments, the words for *breath* and *spirit* are interchangeable. God breathed life into the beings shaped from mud, and Adam and Eve became living creatures. In Ezekiel's vision, "Come from the four winds, O breath" is also translated, "Come from the four winds, O spirit." In Luke 8:55, a young girl dies even as her family seeks help from Jesus. When Jesus arrives at her bedside he says, "Child, get up!" Her spirit, her breath, returns to her and she gets up. The breath of God resurrects.

God is as near to us as our breath. Mostly we take breathing for granted. We pay little attention to the average twelve times per minute we inhale and exhale. Yet our breath can be a diagnostic tool for listening to our inner life and physical well-being, for listening to God. Henri Nouwen writes in *Window Toward the World*, "When we speak about the Holy Spirit, we speak about the breath of God, breathing in us." In 1 Corinthians 3:16, Paul asks, "Do you not know that you are God's temple and that God's Spirit dwells in you?" God's Holy Spirit, Holy Breath, dwells in us.

Becoming aware of our breathing invites us to pay attention to God's life-breath, God's spirit, in us. Think for a moment how our breath reflects physical and emotional conditions. We run a race, panting, even gasping, for air. We are anxious, fearful, stressed; our breathing is shallow and quick. We are

Becoming aware of our breathing invites us to pay attention to God's life-breath, God's spirit, in us.

bored or overwhelmed, and we sigh. We are awed by the beauty of a rose and breathe deeply of the heady scent. We struggle to sleep and take ten deep, agonizingly slow breaths, pushing all the air out of our lungs at each exhale, then sink into relaxation. When we turn attention to our breath, inviting ourselves to slow down and breathe deeply, we alter our physical and emotional experience. We invite ourselves to be present with God in the stillness, there to be renewed.

INTEGRATING

1. To care for ourselves, we need to be present to our bodies, to our experiences. Use this exercise to attend to yourself and to God.

> Find a comfortable position. Follow your breathing from the bottom of the exhale to the top of the inhale. Notice the rhythm, the depth, the pace of each breath. Let a word or phrase take shape as you follow your breath, repeating it, allowing it to change until it seems right. Reflect for a moment on the meaning of the word(s) and the connection to your life. Next, shift the focus back to your breathing, this time paying attention to the breath of God, the Spirit, breathing in you. How does your breathing change? What word or phrase comes to mind as you attend to God's breath?

2. What are the dry bones, the desert places, in your circumstances that long for new life, new breath? What areas of your life or world need restoration, reviving? What is your reaction to God's conundrum/puzzle, "Can these bones live?"

3. What is God to you, through your breath, about how to care for yourself in your body, in your work, in your relationships, in your spiritual life? What does it mean to be God's holy temple?

CLOSING

Read together or sing slowly "Breathe on Me, Breath of God" (*Hymnal: A Worship Book* #356). Let your breath sustain each phrase. Between phrases, take a slow, lung-filling breath. Let God's Spirit work and speak through the singing/speaking. End with a minute of silence as the words resonate within.

Songs:
- *Hymnal: A Worship Book* #299, "New earth, heavens new"
- *HWB* #57, "Come and give thanks to the Giver"
- *HWB* #298, "Veni Sancte Spiritus"

two

Self-Care: Delight in Rich Food

READING: Isaiah 55:1-2

OVERVIEW

Isaiah speaks the words of Yahweh to the people of Israel who are exiled in Babylon. The words are those of a street vendor selling food and drink. But this food is available without money—it is free. Not only is water available in this dry, dusty land, but wine and milk, the foods of the rich and powerful, are available free of charge. In this land of captivity, God calls the people to "listen carefully," to "eat what is good," and to "delight" themselves "in rich food." Food that satisfies.

VISUAL: Arrangement of fruits and vegetables, table setting, or picture of elegantly presented meal

GATHERING

On a warm day, I walked out of the YMCA with well-stretched muscles. I breathed in deeply, feeling tired and rejuvenated at the same time. As I crawled into my sun-baked car and thought about lunch, "vegetables" blazed across the my mind. What? Did that thought really come from me? No craving for bread, rice, or pastry? Just *vegetables*? Okay, maybe with a little dressing and some fruit thrown in, too.

Throughout my just-completed exercise class we were instructed to listen to our bodies, to let our bodies be our guide for signs of strain or pain. Focusing on the strengths and limits of our physical ability undergirded each exercise. During the cool-down period, my body relaxed, my thoughts stopped whirring, and I became fully present to my whole self, spent and renewed. Having slowed down and listened to what I deeply needed, I instinctively chose the good, the healthy, the "rich" food.

DEEPENING

The words of God spoken through Isaiah call us to "listen carefully." Foundational to any good, healthy relationship is listening. We listen to the "still small voice" of God, to our spouse, to our children, to our friend. And so it is in relationship to ourselves and eating. We learn to listen to our bodies, to pay attention to when we are hungry or full.

Wisdom resides in the body for right food choices. I remember being surprised that babies, given the right selection of foods, will choose a balanced diet—even if they eat all peas one day, bananas another, and sweet potatoes another. Over the course of a few days they will eat from all the food groups in balance. What happens to this innate ability? As we develop we become more intrigued with the outside world and lose touch with our bodies. To regain this ability, we listen.

God's second directive is to "eat what is good." What is good? We are bombarded by information on food and health. Bookstore shelves are laden with diet and cuisine options, each claiming to be "the guarantee" to healthy living. Every day my web browser carries another report on healthy food choices. "Eat This, Not That!" books proliferate. We know processed foods contain ingredients that are not good for us. A healthy-sounding entree at a restaurant contains hundreds of hidden calories. Yet with our busy lives, convenience is attractive. So much information, so many bewildering choices, may lead us to shut down and give up, or to obsess about calories and ingredients, ad nauseum.

What we need is balance—balance achieved by careful listening to God, to our bodies, and to our emotions.

What we need is balance—balance achieved by careful listening to God, to our bodies, and to our emotions. We need to distinguish between what our bodies need and what our emotions or habits direct us to want.

Our third directive from the Isaiah passage is to "delight in rich food." How often do we take great pleasure in the food we eat? Delighting in food means savoring it, experiencing the smell, the texture, the flavors. Delighting in food is not grabbing a snack on the run, downing fast food in the car, eating at the desk or in front of the television. Maybe the first food group that comes to mind when we think of delight is dessert. Cherry Delight, a childhood favorite, or deep, rich, dark chocolate is even healthy. To delight in our food requires us to slow down, observe with all our senses, and find great satisfaction in the bounteous gifts of God's table.

INTEGRATING

1. In the Isaiah passage, God invites us to listen, then to eat what is good and delight in rich food. Think about a time when you listened to God's voice within regarding food. What message did you hear?

2. How do you recognize the difference between satisfying hungry emotions (stress, boredom, anxiety, depression) and satisfying your physical needs for fuel?

3. The Apostle Paul encourages us with the following words, "So, whether you eat or drink, or whatever you do, do everything for the glory of God" (1 Corinthians 10:31). How does our eating and drinking glorify God?

4. Practice taking delight in your next meal. Artfully arrange the food on your plate. Gaze at the rich colors, textures and details of the items. Breathe in deeply the aromas before you. Listen to your internal need for food. Then take up your fork or spoon and bring a bite slowly to your mouth anticipating the joy to come. Chew the food slowly, savoring tastes and smells, close your eyes and find the great satisfaction that comes from the wondrous source of joy. Speak your delight to God in gratitude for this gift of food.

CLOSING

Serve a simple snack. Take time to observe the food, feel the texture, smell the aroma, in anticipation of eating. As you eat, close your eyes and savor the flavors and textures. Give thanks to God for this delightful gift of food.

Songs:

Hymnal: A Worship Book #91, "Praise to God, immortal praise"
HWB #457, "Be present at our table, Lord"
Sing the Journey #86, "Taste and see"

three . . . .

Self-Care: Walk in the Way

READING: Psalm 25:4-5; Isaiah 30:21; Romans 12:1

OVERVIEW

The texts for this lesson recognize God's interaction with our physical movement in the world. As we seek God's way, God leads, teaches, and speaks to us, telling us the way to walk. The Old Testament contains many references to walking in the way of God—that is, to put feet, or movement, to following the way of God.

Paul's words in Romans call us to view our bodies as holy and acceptable to God. God created human beings in God's own image and pronounced this creation good. God formed the bodies out of clay, then breathed and brought the bodies to life. We are *embodied* creatures. Paul goes on to say that when we give ourselves to God in our bodies, we worship.

These passages point us to find our way in the world through walking, and invite us to understand that giving our holy and acceptable embodied selves to God is an act of worship.

VISUAL: Picture of someone walking a path or highway, walking shoes, excercise equipment/images

GATHERING

Walking in the World by Julia Cameron sat on my bookshelf gathering dust. Selecting resources to take on retreat, I grabbed it, intending to explore my surroundings. During my retreat I took periodic walks. Walking with intention to focus on my spiritual life while attending to physically putting one foot in front of the other, I observed my surroundings at the same time. Encouraged, I used physical movement as a way of prayer and contemplation, but received no great revelation, no whispering of "This is the way; walk in it."

Months later, teaching a class in pastoral care using the creative arts, I engaged the students in a spiritual walking exercise. While they moved around the room and building, I decided to do the exercise as well. With no particular focus in mind, I walked up the steps of the auditorium, wandered through the foyer and outdoors, and tried to come back into the room through another door. Grabbing hold of the door handle I pulled and, nothing! The door did not budge an inch. I was locked out; my way was blocked.

Just because the path is blocked one way does not mean the end of the journey. Another way opens if we keep walking.

Retracing my steps, I drew what I just experienced: the path and the roadblock. Then I struck out on another path. Going up a different stairway, I passed through the locked door from the inside out. My heart beat faster, my adrenaline soared as the insight resonated in my body—just because the path is blocked one way does not mean the end of the journey. Another way opens if we keep walking.

I saw the connection to my life. My husband and I had recently participated in a bidding war in Southern California on the "perfect" house. We lost to the one out of fourteen bidders who paid cash. I felt crushed and discouraged. Shortly after the walking exercise, we found another house that was a far better fit for our family. It truly felt like a miracle find, a gift house from God.

DEEPENING

In the Quaker tradition there is a saying that refers to finding one's path in life: "Way opens." Often we don't know that until we start moving. Isaiah states that it is when we turn to the right or left that we hear God affirming our way. We know the way when we engage our bodies in the process.

Reflecting on Paul's words, there are many ways to present our bodies to God. Engaging our full selves in spiritual worship is one. Whether in a church service, in the gym, or in the grocery store, we can open ourselves to God's presence as we move our bodies through space. What is required is an act of intention and attention, bringing our whole selves, mind and spirit, to the activity of our body. God speaks to us through this avenue.

We are accustomed to using words in our worship. When we involve our bodies in worship, we open ourselves to the rich connection to God that comes through our many senses, not our intellect and verbal ability alone. This is why music and singing are so powerful to our worship experience.

Paul also states that our bodies are holy and acceptable. God created us in God's own image, pronouncing that creation "very good." We are embodied beings, something we often take for granted until we encounter a physical limitation. Owning our bodies as the "temple of the Holy Spirit" brings sacredness to our engagement in everyday activities. Approaching exercise and other health-promoting practices from the perspective of caring for the temple of God encourages our flagging commitment to care for ourselves. There is a holy purpose to our exercise, to our movement. God will meet us here, and "way opens."

INTEGRATING

1. What does it mean for us to reconnect to our bodies? To see them as holy and acceptable? To be embodied persons?

2. Choose a Bible story and act out the scenes. Engage your body in telling the story. How does this affect your interpretation, or the meaning you take with you from the reading?

3. Next time you exercise, give your attention to the way in which your body is a temple for God's presence in you. As you care for and strengthen your body, how does this impact your relationship to God?

4. Take a prayer walk (see "Closing") in your current setting to engage your body in the practice of prayer and listening to God.

CLOSING

Engage in a prayer walk. Take five minutes and begin walking with no destination in mind. Allow your feet to lead you, to stop where they will. Pause and take note of your surroundings. What do you see before you? Let God meet you in this space. Journal, draw, or share your insights with others. May God bless your walking in the way and may "way open."

Songs:

Sing the Journey #78, "Sizohamba naye (We will walk with God)"
Hymnal: A Worship Book #538, "Lead me, Lord"
HWB #45, "I cannot dance, O Love"
HWB #439, "I want Jesus to walk with me"

four . . . .

Self-Care: Rest for Your Souls

READING: Matthew 11:28-29; Psalm 23:2

OVERVIEW

Jesus invites us to bring the burdens and cares of our lives to him for respite—to lay down the struggles, the rules, the cares, the responsibilities, the demands of our lives. When we do, he will give us rest. In the Gospel of John, Jesus refers to himself as the Good Shepherd. God as shepherd is the image from Psalm 23, where God leads David to green pastures and still waters to restore his soul. Following the example of Jesus, learning his ways, taking up the causes that Jesus cares about, will lead us to find rest for our souls.

VISUAL: Pillow and blanket or quilt

GATHERING

At a time when I experienced a high level of stress in my life, a spiritual director led me in a visual exercise. Reflecting on the contributors to my stress, I envisioned them in a huge Santa Claus-type sack, only grey-brown instead of bright red. With the sack hefted onto my back—bulging out in places, unwieldy and heavy—I trudged up a winding, mountainous gravel path with my load. Climbing was slow and the bag cumbersome; all felt impossible.

Along the trail I met a character I acknowledged as Jesus. He lifted the bag from my back, laid it down, and gestured for me to take a rest in a grassy glen by a brook. As I lay back in the sunshine, cool breeze wafting over me, feeling the earth beneath me, the words floated into my mind, "Come to me. I will give you rest. Learn from me; there is the rest for your soul." I knew in that moment I did not have to pick that bag up again. I could leave it where it lay. I didn't have to carry these burdens alone.

DEEPENING

The biblical concept of rest is rooted in the creation story. God creates the universe in six days and rests on the seventh. This sets an example for the Israelites to follow: they are to rest from their labors every seventh day. The adults, the children, the slaves, the livestock, even the strangers living in the towns, all rest on this consecrated day.

We instinctively know we need rest. Recent research indicates we all function best with eight hours of sleep a night, regardless of age. Those of us who take midday power naps are more productive in our workplaces. As a mother, when my son was young, I learned that even though I could accomplish a dozen tasks while he slept, I benefitted more by grabbing a nap.

Dreams during sleep can provide poignant indicators of what we need to attend to in our lives. We know from sleep research that our minds work out problems while we sleep, often resulting in solutions not thought of during the light and stress of day. Fragmented parts suddenly come together, consolidate into an integrated whole.

Consolidation also happens when we pause or take breaks from activities. After practicing for hours on a complicated piano passage I fear I will never master, I can take a break for a day or more, then come back and play the passage perfectly. How does that happen? Truly, we are fearfully and wonderfully made.

Resting invites us to slow down, to attend to what truly matters, to let go of the weighty issues we are shouldering. When we pause . . . we gain perspective and clarity.

Resting invites us to slow down, to attend to what truly matters, to let go of the weighty issues we are shouldering. When we pause from our various activities, we gain perspective and clarity. We gain insight and draw conclusions that otherwise eluded us. We lay down our burdens, the stress we are carrying, the myopic thinking, the slavish commitment to perfection. Jesus invites us to be humble, to accept help, to look to eternal things drawing our attention to God, thus receiving rest for our souls. For when we attend to the truly important, the burdensome quality of our lives fades.

Whether spending time on retreat, sleeping a full eight hours, breathing deeply between classes, soaking in a warm tub, curling up on the sofa, or taking a nap, resting restores our souls to live fully and abundantly.

INTEGRATING

1. What are the ways you rest throughout your day, week, and year?

2. Describe a time when you experienced the lifting of your burden. How did that occur? What were the circumstances?

3. Reflect on your sleep pattern. Do you get enough? Too much? Is there anything you would like to change?

4. Explore ways that you can take a "pause," a break from an activity or life circumstance, that will allow time for reflection and consolidation.

5. Meditate on Psalm 23. You may read it in the spiritual practice of Lectio Divina:

> Read the passage through once. Read the passage a second time, this time allowing a word or phrase to stand out. Spend some time in silence. Read the passage a third time, allowing a feeling or image to stand out. Spend some time in silence. Read the passage a fourth time, this time noting what God is speaking to you personally. Reflect again in silence. (If this exercise is done in a group, you may speak aloud the words, images, and messages from God.)

CLOSING

Prayer:

Surely goodness and mercy shall follow us all the days of our lives, and we shall dwell in the house of the Lord our whole lives long, as we find our rest in God where our souls are restored.

Songs:

Hymnal: A Worship Book #578, "The Lord's my shepherd"
HWB #557, "O God, in restless living"
HWB #5, "There is a place of quiet rest"
Sing the Journey #77, "The peace of the earth be with you"

five . . . .

Self-Care: Seek Wisdom

READING: Proverbs 2:1-5, 9-11

OVERVIEW

The book of Proverbs contains pithy statements and admonitions of Solomon, to whom God gave the gift of wisdom. Solomon imparts wisdom to his children, the descendants of David, and to us. We are entreated to seek wisdom, understanding, and insight as if we are searching for hidden treasure. The pursuit of these things will lead us to the fear of the LORD, the wonder and awe of God, as well as to know God. We are encouraged to make our ears attentive to wisdom, which will enter our very souls to guard and guide our way in the world.

VISUAL: Stack of books, including Bible, representing search for knowledge

GATHERING

You Already Know What to Do. The title jumped out at me as I browsed the shelves of my favorite bookstore in Pasadena, California. Leafing through the pages, I knew this resource would engage me for an upcoming retreat.

Sorting through all the possibilities and personal interests that stream across my consciousness can occupy a lot of time—time spent sifting through the laundry list of tasks and options I could pursue. Prioritizing the have-to-do's from the want-to-do's, often dithering about what's best to do. This is the perpetual dilemma of a high "Perceiving" score on the Myers Briggs Personality Type Indicator—that is, someone who keeps gathering data before making a decision. But this book held out the answer to me: I already know what to do.

All I have to do is access that knowledge. Slow down, go deep within, and listen. This is more easily written than done. Yet, I have come to value this deep listening. Now, after making my "To Do" list, I head my next entry: "Because I'm listening to God's deep wisdom within, I already know to . . ." Then I list no more than ten items. Inevitably, these are the true priorities for a given moment in time. Sometimes the list contains mundane tasks, and sometimes more profound insight.

During the process of writing this Bible study guide, I have returned to this well of wisdom over and over. Selecting Scripture passages, seeking God's movement in my life, discerning critical issues in the lives of women—all gave ample opportunities to tap into the mystery of God, to truly know God and what I am to do.

DEEPENING

The exercises in the book *You Already Know What to Do* by Sharon Franquemont led me to create a collage from randomly selected magazine pictures. The result was a delightful surprise. Seemingly unrelated images held symbols and meaning for specific topics: a mom enjoying her child (nurturing joy), a stand of sequoia trees (cultivating solitude), a piano (discovering purpose). I experienced the benefit of accessing the right brain, where creativity, emotions, relationships, and non-linear thinking reign supreme.

Most of our world is attuned to the highly developed and honed left brain bound by language, structure, and rules. The right hemisphere of our brains contains deep wisdom. Emotional intelligence, lodged here, fundamentally impacts our relationships and our success in a many areas of life. This intelligence is considered critical for successful executives and leaders.

> The right brain connects to the "heart," the seat of emotions, understanding,and wisdom referred to in our Scripture passage.

We engage the right brain when entering solitude and contemplation, gazing at a work of art, making music, drawing, loving. The right brain connects to the "heart," the seat of emotions, understanding, and wisdom referred to in our Scripture passage. It reflects a deep knowing and may not always be explainable in words.

I have had moments of "knowing" in every fiber of my being that the way was clear in my life. I remember driving into Washington, D.C., when applying for an internship and knowing for certain I would be there. I was "home." I've had similar experiences with job interviews, entering new settings, choosing an office for my solo psychotherapy practice. There have been fuzzy moments, too. Yet, as I wait and continue to listen deeply, the way becomes clear. With hindsight I can identify indicators that led to my "knowing," but in the moment the signs are mostly visceral and beyond language.

In this deep wisdom, the space beyond language, we know what to do. Here we meet and know God. "Be still and know that I am God!" (Psalm 46:10). In the still, small voice, God tells us go to the right or to the left. With this wisdom, understanding, and knowledge, we will be prompted to do those things which care for ourselves and lead us to care for others and our world.

INTEGRATING

1. Describe a time when you had a "gut feeling" that turned out to be right. Did you sense the presence of God? What inner wisdom and knowledge was activated in the process?

2. Take a moment to reflect on a current dilemma in your life, a decision you find unclear. Quiet yourself, the internal chatter. Go deep inside and be still. When you are quiet, write on a piece of paper, "Because I am listening to the deep inner wisdom of God, I already know to . . ." Fill in the blank with words or images that flow from the place of peace.

3. How do you determine when you are being pulled by the forces of the world or wants and needs of others, instead of being grounded in God's wisdom? Describe the ways in which you know God's leading.

4. Describe a time when you have been true to yourself, followed your voice, even if it did not seem the most rational thing to do.

CLOSING

Prayer:

O God, *we make our ears attentive to wisdom*
we incline our hearts to understanding,
we cry out for insight and understanding
seeking wisdom like silver
searching for it as hidden treasure.
That we may know the awe, the wonder, the mystery
of you.

Songs:

Hymnal: A Worship Book #303, "Come, gracious Spirit"
HWB #517, "Open my eyes, that I may see"
Sing the Story #65, "Abre mis ojos (Open my eyes)"

six . . . .

Self-Care: Reclaim Childlikeness

READING: Mark 10:13-16

OVERVIEW

In the Gospels, stories abound of women and men flocking to Jesus to be touched and healed, to be freed from demons, to be blessed and made whole. When some bring children for Jesus to touch, the disciples scold them and seek to send the children away. The ministry of Jesus is serious business, for adults only, they believe. Jesus, indignant at this action, welcomes the children, holds them, and blesses them. He tells the adults they must become like little children to receive and enter the kingdom of God.

VISUAL: Picture of child or children, toys and playthings

GATHERING

Morning came early on Sunday, the day of Sabbath rest. Entering the chapel, more aptly called a cathedral, I slipped into a back row so as not to cause a disturbance. I fully intended to stay in my pew, but was surprised at the urgency I felt as the rows in front of me emptied into the aisle to take communion. The officiating priest said nothing to indicate the sacraments were only for baptized, catechized members of the congregation.

I joined the line, next to a family walking down the long aisle. As I reached the priest, hands cupped to receive the bread, he reached out his hand to rub the heads of the two young boys next to me, pronouncing words of blessing. Tears sprang to my eyes. As I put the dry, papery wafer on my tongue, I knew I would have preferred the blessing.

What made that action so poignant to me? Some part of me longed to be taken into the arms of Jesus, to become a child again and know the fullness of life and love received unconditionally. I wanted to be touched, hugged, and blessed with deep acceptance and appreciation, to regain the wonder and awe, the freedom of childlikeness. I wanted to be welcomed, valued, and loved just for who I am, a child of God.

DEEPENING

During most of my life, I have identified with the scolding disciples in this passage more than with Jesus or the little children. Following the rules, doing what's right, not interrupting or putting others out—these were values I learned growing up. The scolding disciples' voices are alive and well in my head: "Don't interrupt," "Don't put yourself forward," "Don't cause a commotion," "Be seen but not heard." On and on the critical voices continue, especially if I'm getting too excited about anything.

As little children we are curious, open, accepting, exuberant and maybe reticent, exploring and engaging our world. Through learning how to behave in our families, school, and church, we curb much of our free-spirited nature. For women, this occurs most profoundly around the age of nine years. "Sit up straight," "Keep your legs together," "Use your 'inside' voice," "Don't romp around like a wild animal," are messages we internalize. While maturity and manners are good things, we sometimes confuse training and restraint with cutting off and extinguishing vital parts of our being. The critical voice gains strength over the free-wheeling exploration and excitement of the child.

While maturity and manners are good things, we sometimes confuse training and restraint with cutting off and extinguishing vital parts of our being.

Attending to our childlikeness grants us the ability to enter the kingdom of God. Further, it can serve to quiet the scolding, critical internal voice. From a psychological perspective, the critical voice carries the corrections, limitations, and sometimes even abuses, that we received from caregivers and others throughout our lives. The critical voice attempts to keep us from getting into trouble, from experiencing the shame or disturbance caused by our wrong-doing. That is the positive role. However, there is a downside. Too much criticism results in squelched energy, enthusiasm, and genuine creativity. Joy can turn into fear, curiosity into inhibition, dancing into tapping toes.

John, in his first letter, talks about the breadth and depth of God's love for us, God's children. As the beloved of God, he states, "There is no fear in love, but perfect love casts out fear" (1 John 4:18a). Feeling loved and valued by God, by others, and by ourselves leads us to a sense of serenity and security that promotes self-worth. Self-worth, in turn, helps us approach our work, our relationships, our caregiving, and our worship with greater sense of well-being. We are more confident. We are more joyful. We dance. Our cup is full and runs over as we engage the world.

INTEGRATING

1. Jesus invites us to receive the kingdom of God as a little child. What does this mean for us? How do we reconnect with the child within?

2. How do you play? Where do you find fun and enjoyment in life? What toys have you kept from your childhood?

3. What messages did you hear growing up that now inhibit you as an adult? What do the scolding disciples in your head say to keep you from going after what you want?

4. Describe a time you felt valued, loved, and accepted with warmth and welcoming, either by others or by God. How did this affect your outlook on life? Your actions in the world?

CLOSING

Prayer:

Lord, help us to become like little children in our exuberance and excitement to be blessed by you. Help us to seek you and your kingdom with wonder and awe, with the confidence of knowing we are loved, valued, and welcomed. Help us to love others and ourselves with this same freedom and abandonment, restoring joy and well-being. May it be so.

Songs:

Hymnal: A Worship Book #167, "For God so loved us"
HWB #620, "Child of blessing, child of promise"
HWB #621, "Jesus, friend so kind and gentle"
HWB #427, "You shall go out with joy"

seven . . . .

Self-Care: Share Burdens

READING: Galatians 6:2

OVERVIEW

Paul admonishes the Galatian Christians to support one another through difficult times. Particularly, in the context of this verse, he calls fellow believers to gently restore a person who transgresses the law of Christ in some way. In the gentle bearing of another's burdens, we fulfill the law of Christ, recognizing our own human frailties even as we hold up another who is struggling.

VISUAL: Small table with two chairs, two cups and saucers

GATHERING

For years, praying was nearly impossible for me. I felt no connection to God. Life had taken a turn I did not understand, and I wandered in a spiritual wilderness. Going through the motions of faithfulness, I attended church, led worship and music, offered God's hope to my psychotherapy clients, all the while feeling abandoned by God.

In the Old Testament, Hannah cried out to God her frustrated desire to have a child. Eli the priest heard her cries, as did

God, who fulfilled her longing. But my cries fell on deaf ears. No pregnancy occurred; no child emerged. Eventually, the tears wrung out of me left nothing but numbness.

"Sing, O barren one who did not bear; burst into song and shout . . . For the children of the desolate woman will be more than the children of her that is married, says the Lord" (Isaiah 54:1). *Sing, O Barren One* was the title of a book my husband encountered in his theological studies. Handing the book to me became a gentle restoration even as we struggled together through the heartbreak of infertility. Studying and working with this Scripture led me to look beyond the immediate devastation of unfulfilled longings and dreams to what God might do in spite of our current barrier.

During the next couple of years my heart was opened to explore meanings and possibilities not previously considered. I still found it hard to offer prayers of petition to God; I expected no answer. Yet, at the same time, new vistas of God's direction and calling spread before me.

After the birth and adoption of our son, I heard the following words repeatedly from many sources: "I've been praying for you, and God answered my prayer." Unknown to me, many friends, family, and church members held me in prayer daily, even when I could barely face God. They carried my burden and in the process restored my relationship to God. A humbling and buoyant feeling undergirded my euphoria in receiving our son. I was never abandoned. Love and care surrounded me all through that wilderness.

DEEPENING

At times in our lives, we confront our own limits. We do not have the strength or will, the physical or psychic resources to accomplish what we need to do, to withstand a temptation, or to face a trial. At these times we lose faith and hope. This is when we need the body of Christ to share our burden.

Reading Paul's entreaty to the Galatians to bear one another's burdens, we most often focus on the aspect of taking on the burden of another—stepping in to help, as Simon of Cyrene was compelled to do in carrying the cross for Jesus to Golgotha. We think of taking a meal to someone who is sick, going shopping for an invalid, rebuilding a home that has been destroyed, or listening to someone who is grieving. We usually look at this text from the "giving" end.

Holding hope for someone who feels no hope is a sacred trust.

Holding hope for someone who feels no hope is a sacred trust. There are times I have done this for psychotherapy clients who could not see beyond their current struggle or devastating situation. Because I had been held in prayer and hope through my own "valley," I could offer to hold hope with confidence that sharing the burden of another would restore vision and functioning. Faith would be renewed.

Allowing ourselves to be carried, our burdens to be shared, is an act of self-care. Sometimes we push ourselves beyond our limits when it would be better to stop and accept the help of a caring sister. Asking for help may make us feel weak, powerless, even ashamed. For if God's grace is sufficient, shouldn't we be able to handle everything that comes our way? The body of Christ is God's grace to us. And so, we offer God's grace to one another.

Prayers are a way we bear one another's burdens, as proved true for me through my infertility crisis. Even now, as I write, I'm wearing a prayer shawl knitted with prayers by a woman from Berne, Indiana. The shawl was bestowed upon me at a

Sister Care seminar in Ohio by my table group, for my work in writing this Bible study guide. Wrapped in the prayers of these women gives me strength to persevere, even when the going gets rough. Let us share our burdens with one another.

INTEGRATING

1. Reflect on a time when you reached a limit within yourself that required you to look to another for help. What was the experience like? How did the help come to you?

2. Describe a time in your life when you carried the burden for another. How did God empower you to have hope for that person? What was the outcome?

3. Reflect on an experience you have had in either praying for someone or being prayed for that resulted in transformation or healing.

4. Three verses after Paul encourages believers to bear one another's burdens, he states that "all must carry their own loads." How do these two conflicting notions impact you?

CLOSING

Stand in a circle or face each other and sing "Will You Let Me Be Your Servant" (*Hymnal: A Worship Book* #307). Alternate verses between groups, allowing each to experience offering and receiving support. For the final verse, you may choose to sing, "*I will let you* be my servant . . ."

Songs:

Sing the Journey #87, "Put peace into each other's hands"
STJ #69, "Cuando el pobre (When the poor ones)"
Hymnal: A Worship Book #305, "Where charity and love prevail"
HWB #420, "Heart with loving heart united"

eight . . . .

Self-Care: Do Not Worry

Reading: Matthew 6:25-34

OVERVIEW

Many are seeking Jesus to heal their diseases and cure their illnesses. Crowds follow him on his travels. His fame has spread throughout Syria, Galilee, Jerusalem, Judea, and beyond the Jordan river. Jesus seeks refuge with his disciples from the massive crowd and begins to teach them on the mountain. The Beatitudes, love for enemies, giving of alms, and the Lord's Prayer are delivered in this context. Within this Sermon on the Mount, Jesus exhorts his disciples, and subsequently us, not to worry. He points us to the lilies and the birds—elements of nature that God cares for, clothes, and feeds. God also cares about our needs and supplies them. We don't need to bring more trouble into our day by worrying about tomorrow.

VISUAL: Lily plant or bouquet of daylillies

GATHERING

Clothes are hanging at every available spot in my closet and bedroom as I try on various combinations to create just the right ensemble. Proportion, color, and texture either work or they do not: One pair of shoes with one pair of slacks, but no others. Scarves thrown about in an attempt to coordinate disparate parts. Every time I prepare for a trip, I go through this major process. How can I have a closet and drawers full of clothes and still have nothing to wear?

Well, yes, my size does fluctuate from time to time. And now I have to deal with four seasons, not a problem for 26 years in Southern California. That jacket that looked so right in the store dressing room just doesn't work with what I have. Not to mention that finding versatile pieces to complement my coloring, my proportions, and my budget is no small feat.

I can work myself into a frenzy trying to find just the right top or shoes or coat. Once I'm on my way I wonder, what was all that fretting about?

I can work myself into a frenzy trying to find just the right top or shoes or coat. Of course, no store carries exactly what I envision, so I have to settle for something less than perfect. And there are a number of "less than perfect" fashion statements clogging my closet.

Once I'm on my way with suitcase packed, all that craziness subsides. I'm wearing the same shoes I've worn the last five years, because nothing else comes close to their comfort and versatility. And I wonder, what was all that fretting about?

There are two lessons here. One, planning earlier means less frenzy. Two, ultimately, what I wear is not me, even if it is an expression of myself. What matters is who I am and how I am with others. Living in the moment, the here and now, is more beneficial than all my consternation about what to wear. God knows what I need and supplies it when required.

DEEPENING

Jesus addresses three areas of worry in the Matthew 6 passage: what to eat, what to drink, and what to wear. These represent the basics of life, not the extras. The lesson from the birds and the lilies is that God takes care of the basics. We are to strive for the kingdom of God and all God's righteousness. If we put our energy into pursuing God, we won't be sucked dry by worrying about the future. All that we need will be provided.

One struggle we face in self-care is separating what we need from what we want. I *want* the Death by Chocolate cake. I *need* the Honeycrisp apple. I *want* the caramel macchiato. I *need* water. I *want* the perfect outfit. I *need* what is "good enough."

There is an important difference between worry and healthy anxiety. A certain amount of anxiety is needed to push us forward, to finish a project, to take a risk, to study for an exam. Yet, too much anxiety results in circular thinking, immobilization from tackling the task at hand, imagining outcomes that are not realistic or even catastrophic. We then begin to live in the future, instead of in the moment, borrowing tomorrow's trouble for today.

In the Bible story, people are seeking Jesus to heal a disease—paralysis, epilepsy, demon possession. People long to have their basic needs met for nutrition, hydration, and health. In this context of great need, Jesus tells his disciples that God provides the basics. All our worrying will do nothing to alter our lives. Instead, we are to trust in God. Luke's account of this story relates how Jesus then sends his disciples to various places in Judea with nothing but the clothing on their backs and shoes on their feet. Through this experience they learn to trust God for their needs of shelter, food, money, and clothing.

Paul calls for the followers of Christ to "not worry about anything" (Philippians 4:6). Rather, believers are to seek God with prayer, supplication, and thanksgiving. As we do this, we are promised that the peace of God will fill and sustain us.

INTEGRATING

1. What things do you find yourself worrying about the most? How do you handle your worry? Describe a time when you relinquished your worry to God. What was the outcome?

2. How do you distinguish anxiety that motivates from worrying about things you cannot control? What are helpful ways of handling this type of anxiety?

3. Take time to gaze at a lily or other flower, or go birdwatching. Contemplate God's care for these elements of nature. Let the words of Jesus sink in—"Are you not of more value than they?" Submit any worry you may be harboring to God's care.

CLOSING

Prayer:

Help us, O God, not to worry about tomorrow,
but to seek you in everything so that
The peace of God, which surpasses all understanding,
will guard our hearts and our minds in Jesus Christ.

Songs:

Hymnal: A Worship Book #562, "Nada te turbe"
Sing the Journey #77, "The peace of the earth be with you"
Sing the Story #16, "Peace before us"

nine . . . .

Self-Care: Be Cleansed

READING: Psalm 51:1-2, 10

OVERVIEW

Wash me. Cleanse me. These are the words of David, seeking God's mercy after his seduction of Bathsheba. Knowing his guilt and the justified consequences for his actions, he beseeches God to change him through washing, cleansing, and purging (v. 7). Cleansing from sin is represented by the water baptism performed by John the Baptist in preparing the way for the ministry of Jesus. Washing or dipping in water is used to heal physical ailments throughout the Scriptures: Naman dips in the Jordan River and emerges healed from leprosy; the lame and blind who dip or wash in the pool of Siloam are healed. David hopes for a clean heart, a new and right spirit as a result of his cleansing. Until there is cleansing, purging, and repenting, the new cannot come.

VISUAL: Basin and pitcher with towel

GATHERING

Since I began writing this Bible study guide on self-care, I have accomplished a number of cleaning and organizing tasks that would otherwise remain undone. It's amazing what avoiding hard work in one arena motivates us to do in another!

You could call this procrastination or distraction, and you would be right. Certainly I am not working on the project at hand. However, inevitably, while I'm rearranging kitchen cupboards, putting up shelves, finding homes for things that have cluttered the garage for the last four years, or even sweeping off the deck, new insights come to me.

As I raked leaves one morning, I thought of a well-published author's words, as I remember them: "There's no such thing as inspiration or writer's block, there's only 'butt in chair' time." So here I am, putting in my "bic" time, whether I feel inspired or blocked. At least the leaves are off the lawn.

Sometimes the physical activity of cleansing tasks—bathing, cleaning house, purging a closet or junk drawer, filing—frees our minds to focus on more complex matters. This opens us to the new God has for us. We can experience internal cleansing and renewing even as we participate in the other tasks.

I discovered in writing about self-care that I have used a number of self-care practices to clear what plugs up my life and energy and keeps me blocked. Putting myself to the task of clearing out old thoughts and feelings as well as material "stuff" creates space for new understanding, insight, and other blessings of God.

DEEPENING

What is it about the act of cleaning or organizing that sparks new accomplishments? When we clean out the old, we make way for the new to come to us. As people repented of their sins in the desert and were baptized with water by John the Baptist, it made the way for Jesus to come, to teach and to baptize with the Holy Spirit and with fire. Water baptism prepared the people, softening their hearts for new thoughts,

> We can think of our acts of cleaning, bathing, purging, as outward signs of our inward transformation. They remind us of God's work in our lives.

new insights, and a whole new way of life brought by Jesus. Remember the story of Saul, who had persecuted the early followers of Jesus. After Saul's conversion to become a proclaimer of the good news of Jesus, Ananias encouraged him to be baptized. This gave an outward sign of his drastic inward change as his name was changed from Saul to Paul.

Purging and pruning are also concepts of making way for the new, found throughout the Scriptures. The same root is used in Greek for both *pruning* and *cleansing*: pruning the branches so the fruit can spring forth (John 15:1-3), putting off the old things, the old ways of living (Ephesians 4:22-24), and making room for the new fruits of the Spirit to blossom and flourish (Galatians 5:22-25).

We can think of our acts of cleaning, bathing, purging, as outward signs of our inward transformation. For indeed, when the floors are shining, when the counter is cleared off, when clothes are hung and stacked neatly, we breathe more easily. We feel a surge of energy that is missing when everything is piled around us. These simple cleansing acts remind us of God's work in our lives—refashioning us into the gifts God created us to be. We are freed to be refreshed and regenerated with a clean heart and a renewed spirit.

INTEGRATING

1. Reflect on a time when you engaged in a cleansing task and the feelings that accompanied the completion of the task. What new resulted from your efforts?

2. David sought God's forgiveness for his transgression with Bathsheba, asking for a clean heart and right spirit. How have you experienced God's forgiveness and cleansing in your life?

3. When you reflect on pruning or cutting back a garden to allow for new growth, how does that compare with purging in your life to allow the fruits of the Spirit to burst forth?

4. Take a shower or bath sometime when you are feeling immobilized and allow the running water and bathing ritual to clear your mind and heart. Experience renewal in washing away the old, making way for the new. Or purge your closet, clean out a junk drawer, or file a stack of papers. Invite God's presence in your purging.

CLOSING

Prayer:

Have mercy on us, O God,
your love is steadfast and abundant.
Cleanse us from all unrighteousness.
As we go through our daily tasks of cleansing and purging
may our hearts and spirits be made new.

(You may want to use a basin of water and a towel for a hand-washing ritual as part of the closing.)

Songs:

Hymnal: A Worship Book #504, "Have thine own way"
HWB #373, "Thou true Vine, that heals"
HWB #372, "O healing river"
Sing the Journey #82, "Water has held us"
Sing the Story #62, "Create in me a clean heart"

ten . . . .

Self-Care: Nurture Creativity

READING: Exodus 31:1-11; Genesis 1:27-28a

OVERVIEW

God gifts humans with capacities and skills to create. We are made in the image of God, the Creator, and reflect God's image as we create. The Scriptures give countless examples of human creativity in poetry, songs, artifacts, dramatic retelling of stories, and expression of ideas. King David plays the harp, sings, and writes poetry as well as rules Israel. Solomon builds an extravagantly beautiful temple. In the Exodus text, we are told God gifts the artisans who build and adorn the first meeting place of the Israelites—the tabernacle. The arts and creative endeavors are God-given and God-blessed.

VISUAL: Work of art, or art and craft materials (palette and paints, quilting materials, knitting needles)

GATHERING

Peace washes over me as I step through the portals onto the rolling green, palm-tree-studded grounds of The Huntington Library and Gardens. Leaving the cares of my day behind, my soul feasts on the visual delights before me. I can see the ocean far off. When I turn around, the majestic expanse of the San Gabriel mountains anchors my vista. God's creation is awe-inspiring.

The artistic touch of human hands turns God's creation into a bonsai tree, koi pond, desert expanse, rose garden, or gushing waterfall. Architecture, sculptures, paintings, thousands of books attest to more human artistry that reflects on the world God set in motion. Time and space shift for me here as I connect to beauty and things larger than myself. I am inspired to think higher thoughts, to dream grander dreams, to let the "peace of Christ" rule my heart. And to create beauty in my own way.

In her book, *The Artist's Way: A Spiritual Path to Higher Creativity*, Julia Cameron encourages readers to make regular dates with their creative selves. Exploring shops, galleries, natural environments, other places that allow new vistas and ideas to flourish is the goal. Following this suggestion started my weekly visits to the Huntington, where my soul was repeatedly restored over many years. Creative ideas would flow for gardening, resolving conflicts, meeting parenting challenges, planning worship services, writing . . . the list goes on.

A two-pronged process works here. First, entering into environments that nourish our souls and inspire us to be creative brings joy to our lives. Second, using our creativity connects us to Creator God and aids us in experiencing life abundantly.

DEEPENING

We start our lives as creative beings. Childhood is full of imaginary games: building block houses, managing doll families, flying airplanes, playing dress up. As children, we dream big dreams and believe ourselves capable of being anything we imagine—Superwoman, doctor, princess, astronaut. No barriers hinder free-running ideas: crayons on the wall, mom's high-heeled shoes, soap suds in the tub. Our world is our artist's canvas.

As we connect to our sense of wonder, awe, curiosity, uninhibited freedom, and play, we also connect to a God-given capacity to create.

That is, until someone tells us we should color inside the lines. Whether at school or at home, efforts are made to shape our creative endeavors into recognizable shapes and realizable goals. We begin to second-guess ourselves and trust our inner artist less. Often, by adulthood, we have capped our creativity, thinking it is only for the designated artists among us, like the two identified in the Exodus passage, Bezalel and Oholiab.

While God identifies these two as having specific skills, the text goes on to express God's words, "I have given skill to all the skillful." In this passage, the skills refer to those required for building and decorating the tabernacle. I believe we can expand that meaning to include all of us and any skills we possess. Behind our skills are creative ideas and imaginings.

Ponder for a moment the entreaties found in both the Old and New Testament for us to be fruitful, to bear fruit. The image suggests that life and growth spring forth from some creative, generative place within us. Staying with this metaphor, it becomes imperative for us to create, for how else are we to bear fruit? The fruits of our labor are to benefit the world.

Nurturing our creativity is closely linked to reclaiming our childlikeness (session 6). As we connect to our sense of wonder, awe, curiosity, uninhibited freedom, and play, we also connect to a God-given capacity to create. We are living out our God-image in human form as co-creators with God. What new invention, strategy, business, cure for illness, or parenting technique might result from our willingness to expand our horizons? to look beyond what is, to what could be?

INTEGRATING

1. What images come to mind when you read the text describing God's gifts to Bezalel and Oholiab? What are your experiences of the intersection between artists and Christianity in general, or the church in particular?

2. What were your favorite ways of creating as a child? Have you lost any of these? Have you held on to some?

3. How do you use your creativity in everyday life? In your relationships? In your work? In your spiritual life?

4. Use crayons or paints, tear paper and glue it, make a collage or use other art media to play as you explore your creative energy. No rules apply. Let God speak to you through this process.

CLOSING

Prayer:

O Lord, you have filled us with divine spirit, with ability, intelligence and knowledge to create. You have given skills to us. May we join you in bringing beauty and hope to our world through our creativity.

Songs:

Hymnal: A Worship Book #414, "God, who stretched"
HWB #51, "Let the whole creation cry"

eleven . . . .

Self-Care: Rekindle the Gift

READING: 1 Timothy 4:14-15;
2 Timothy 1:4-7, 14

OVERVIEW

Paul writes letters of encouragement to Timothy, a young leader in the ministry of Christ. "Hold firm; remain steady; carry on the ministry tasks in the face of obstacles" dominates the message. Paul reminds Timothy that he has been recognized by God, by Paul, and by the community of faith as holding a gift from God. As a good mentor, Paul bolsters Timothy's flagging zeal of youth as conflicts and struggles arise. Timothy's gift is not to be set aside, but rather carried on in "a spirit of power and of love and of self-discipline." The exercise of the gift brings life, healing, and salvation to those who are touched by Timothy. The gift is not for Timothy alone, but is to be shared.

VISUAL: Collage of diverse women or a beautifully wrapped gift box

GATHERING

I was at an all-time low in my struggle with infertility, feeling battered, bruised, abandoned, and hopeless. Without achieving this goal of procreation, where was the meaning and purpose in my life? I asked. What was the reason for my being?

While meditating I stumbled upon this Scripture—"rekindle the gift"—and felt compelled to understand the deeper meaning behind the infertility. What gift in me could be rekindled? I knew I had to address the growing distance I felt from God. Anger and tears poured forth as I expressed my disappointment, loss, and feeling that I really did not matter to God, or anyone.

As I cried and ranted, a vision came to me of being held close, my hair stroked, and the soothing words, "Let it all out," spoken. God prefers my raving anger and lashing out to my more usual pattern of turning away and shutting down or throwing myself into everyday tasks. In that moment, I knew God had been with me every step of the way, even when I did not sense God's presence.

Then came the clincher. Gently, God reminded me of all the good things in my life, for which I am grateful, and that I matter to God, whether I feel it or not. Deeper yet, God has gifted me with abilities no one else has: gifts of healing, loving, and caring that are uniquely mine to share. These gifts are bestowed on me by divine power and what I do with them is of utmost importance. I walked away from this encounter with renewed awareness that my role as a therapist is truly God's calling and gift of grace to others. Living out that calling as a midwife of the soul, I help others live life abundantly out of their God-given gifted-ness. My own life is fulfilled.

DEEPENING

God has graced each of us with a gift that is uniquely ours to share with the world. No two people have the same experiences, temperament, or environmental factors that shape us.

Each of us was "knit together" (Psalm 139:13) in the womb, designed and created as unique, special, and valuable.

Some of us have many talents and abilities. Some of us have one or two things we know we do well. Recognizing our God-gift connects us to the mission, the ministry, to which God calls us.

> While the gift involves a talent, ability, or capacity that we possess, in reality the gift is *us*.

Often we think of mission or ministry as belonging solely to persons who are ordained to serve God and the church. Indeed, that is part of Timothy's situation—he is an ordained minister of Christ. Yet, from biblical stories, we know that ordinary people played instrumental roles in furthering the work of God throughout Israel's history: Mary, the mother of Jesus; fishermen Peter and James; Deborah, the judge.

God calls us to give out of what we have and who we are. Having received God's gift, the work of our lives is to grow, attend to, and develop the gift—to live it out in the full expression of our lives. While the gift involves a talent, ability, or capacity that we possess, in reality the gift is *us*. The gift is YOU—your personhood in its totality.

We find many reasons to shy away from the prospect of being God's gift to the world, for who are we to presume our lives in this world matter? Yet, this is precisely what Paul points to for Timothy. In 1 Timothy he states, "Don't neglect the gift," which is important for Timothy's own salvation as well as for those who hear his words.

Whether we preach, teach, or mother, or cook, or clean, we do all for the glory of God. In the generous outpouring of our gifts, the world is healed and so are we.

INTEGRATING

1. List ten things that are strengths or gifts you possess. What do others admire in you? What is something you might do if you were ten times bolder?

2. Describe a way in which you have benefited from the gift of someone else's life.

3. Has there been a time in your life when you felt far from God, when the demands of life or the task at hand seemed far greater than your ability? How did encouragement or support to persevere come to you?

4. Identify a time when you were living in the "flow" of your particular gift, where time becomes nonexistent and all else fades into the background. How did you experience the spirit of power, love, and self-discipline in that moment?

CLOSING

Prayer:

May we not neglect the gift that is in us
may we rekindle this gift of God.
May we be freed from any spirit of cowardice,
so we may live fully in your spirit of
power, love and self-discipline, O God.

Songs:

Hymnal: A Worship Book #383, "God, whose giving"
HWB #304, "There are many gifts"
Sing the Journey #72, "One is the body"
STJ #81, "Take, O take me as I am"

twelve . . . .

Self-Care: Write the Vision

READING: Luke 4:18-19, 42-44; Habakkuk 2:2b

OVERVIEW

Jesus gives his first public address recorded by Luke in the synagogue of Nazareth, his hometown. He reads a passage from the scroll of Isaiah of one being anointed by the Spirit of the Lord to bring good news, release captives, heal the blind, and allow the oppressed to go free. Following this reading, Jesus says, "Today this scripture has been fulfilled in your hearing," declaring Isaiah's words his own mission statement.

When driven out of his hometown, Jesus moves on to Galilee to teach and heal. He invites Peter and Andrew to follow him, and his ministry flourishes. People come from all over to be cured of diseases and cleansed from unwholesome spirits. In this context, Jesus gets up at daybreak and goes to a deserted place. The crowd finds him and tries to detain him. Jesus is clear about his next steps. Re-grounded in his mission, he must move on to proclaim the good news to other localities.

In Habakkuk, God instructs the prophet to write down the vision on tablets, so that a runner can carry the message far and wide, keeping it ever front and center.

VISUAL: Copy of mission statement of Mennonite Women USA, Mennonite Women Canada, your denomination, or your church

GATHERING

As I developed a psychotherapy practice, I learned the importance of having a clear vision and plan. This became crucial when I opened my own business after being with a group. Who was my target population? Where would I advertise? What were the best referral sources? How would I pay the rent? A good business and marketing plan became the guidepost for me as I pursued this dream. Lo and behold, I became a sole practitioner and business owner.

All was going well, until I hit a bump in the road, a crossroads—not in my professional life, but in my personal life. My struggle with infertility caused me to question my identity and the meaning and purpose of my life. Even after gaining a renewed sense of my therapy role as a "midwife of the soul," and after becoming a mother through adoption, I was still searching for a mission, a plan for my life as a whole. That's when I was introduced by a colleague in Mennonite Women to *The Path* by Laurie Beth Jones.

Through this resource I developed a mission statement that encompasses the broad range of my life. Family decisions, work decisions, decorating decisions, relationship decisions, and church decisions are guided by the compass of this statement. Rooted in an awareness of my strengths, a clarification of what I value highly, and a clear sense of God's gift in me, my mission statement provides a clarion call to my purpose, a touchstone of God's grace in me.

Like the words of Isaiah that Jesus claimed as his own, my statement is short, easily memorized and repeated. And as

Habakkuk was instructed, I have written down the vision. My mission is:

to heal wounds,
to touch souls,
to create beauty,
and to inspire vital and creative living
in those around me.

DEEPENING

Jesus was clear about his mission from the start. The gospels of Matthew, Mark, and Luke mark his preparation for public ministry with John the Baptist's baptism of Jesus. Subsequently, Jesus enters the wilderness for 40 days and nights, where his mission is honed through the trials of the Tempter. Emerging from this crucible, he begins his ministry that fulfills the words of Isaiah read in the synagogue at Nazareth—teaching, healing, freeing people from oppression. Crowds flock to him, seeking his words and his healing touch.

Highly sought after by others and needed desperately by some, Jesus seems to sense a crossroads, a need to make a decision, that takes him to a deserted place early in the morning. Here he gains clarity and courage to pursue the vision of how to carry out his mission. He must move on to other places, not become a fixture in one location, as people wished and as he may have been tempted to do.

Whether beginning an endeavor or facing an obstacle or crossroads, having a clear mission statement gives us a sense of purpose and direction. Mission statements are not just for organizations. They are highly beneficial for us as individuals. When I am contemplating a request to join a committee, take a new job, or add another assignment to my plate, referring to my mission statement keeps me centered on what I'm called to do. It reflects *how* I will work out my best gifts.

Writing a statement keeps the vision ever before us, no matter where we travel or what opportunities come our way, and empowers us to stay the course. As Jesus needed to stay on task, so must we.

INTEGRATING

1. What images or thoughts come to mind as you reflect on Jesus reading the Isaiah passage and the subsequent path of his life? What lessons do you take from this for your own life?

2. Describe a time when you had a clear vision of what you wanted to accomplish (a quilt design, a vacation, a dinner party . . .) and how you carried out that vision. Are there other ways you would like to employ this process in your life?

3. Take time to write down the dreams you have for yourself. Write them specifically and in the present tense as if they have already occurred. Say, as Jesus did, "Today this [vision] has been fulfilled." Let it incubate and see what God and you do with your dreams.

(See page 63 for guidelines for writing a mission statement.)

CLOSING

Prayer:

The Spirit of God is upon us. May we, young and old, see visions and dream dreams. May we fulfill the call to be lights in the world in which we live and serve.

Song:

Hymnal: A Worship Book #541, "How clear is our vocation, Lord" thirteen . . . .

Fearfully and Wonderfully Made

VISUAL FOCUS

Display a picture of an infant, or an infant hand clasping an adult hand—an image that evokes awe and wonder of God's creation.

GATHERING

Reader 1: As we celebrate the culmination of our lessons in self-care, we give honor and glory to God.

Reader 2: We have learned to listen to God and to ourselves as we breathe, delight in food, walk in the way, cleanse and rest.

Reader 1: We have been encouraged to seek wisdom like hidden treasure, to share our burdens, and to release our worries.

Reader 2: We have been challenged to reclaim our childlikeness so we may enter the kingdom of God, and to nurture our creativity.

Reader 1: Blessed by God with unique and special gifts, we seek to live out our own God-given mission to bring hope and healing to the world.

PRAISING

Call to worship

Leader: Let us bless the Lord at all times.

People: Let us praise God continually with our mouths.

Leader: Let our souls boast in the Lord, so those who are humble may be glad.

People: Let us magnify the Lord and exalt God's name together.

Songs:

Hymnal: A Worship Book #89, "For the beauty of the earth"
HWB #76, "Je lourerai l'Eternel (Praise, I will praise you, Lord)"
Sing the Journey #12, "O sing to the Lord"

GIVING THANKS

Scripture: Psalm 138:1-3, 8

I give you thanks, O Lord, with my whole heart;
before the gods I sing your praise;
I bow down toward your holy temple and give thanks to your name for your steadfast love and your faithfulness;
for you have exalted your name and your word above everything.
On the day I called, you answered me, you increased my strength of soul.
The Lord will fulfill his purpose for me;
your steadfast love, O Lord, endures forever.
Do not forsake the work of your hands.

Songs:

HWB #161, "We give thanks unto you"
STJ #44, "The love of God"

CONFESSION

Litany of confession: *HWB* #690

Songs:
HWB #144, "Kyrie eleison"
STJ #47, "Oh, Lord have mercy"

LISTENING

Scripture: Psalm 139:1-3, 6

O Lord, you have searched me and known me. You know when I sit down and when I rise up; you discern my thoughts from far away. You search out my path and my lying down, and are acquainted with all my ways. Such knowledge is too wonderful for me; it is so high that I cannot attain it.

Silent reflection

Song:
STJ #29, "You are all we have"

Scripture: Psalm 139:13-14

For it was you who formed my inward parts; you knit me together in my mother's womb. I praise you, for I am fearfully and wonderfully made. Wonderful are your works; that I know very well.

Silent reflection

Song:
STJ #29, "You are all we have"

Scripture: Psalm 139:17-18

How weighty to me are your thoughts, O God! How vast is the sum of them! I try to count them—they are more than the sand; I come to the end—I am still with you.

Silent reflection

Song:
STJ #29, "You are all we have"

RESPONDING

Sharing and prayer

Litany of response (*Group responds with phrase in italics.*)

Reader 1: You have met us here in this time and in this place,

for your steadfast love endures forever.

Reader 2: You know us intimately from before we were formed in the womb and hold us close to your heart,

for your steadfast love endures forever.

Reader 1: You have heard our confession, received our broken and contrite hearts, and renewed our spirits,

for your steadfast love endures forever.

Reader 2: You have breathed life into our dry bones and blessed us with rich food in which we take delight,

for your steadfast love endures forever.

Reader 1: You teach us to walk in your way, desire our holy and acceptable bodies to be presented in worship, and grant us rest for our souls,

for your steadfast love endures forever.

Reader 2: You welcome us as little children, blessing us with your unquenchable love,

for your steadfast love endures forever.

Reader 1: You encourage us to lay aside our worries and trust you to provide our needs; you desire us to share our burdens with one another,

for your steadfast love endures forever.

Reader 2: You gift us with creativity, with skills, with a mission to bring hope and healing to the world,

for your steadfast love endures forever.

CLOSING

Benediction:

Go now, in the spirit of power, of love, and of self-discipline
that God has poured out on you,
tending carefully the gift of God you are,
as you live life abundantly, fruitfully, and joyfully,
secure in God's unfathomable love.

Songs:

STJ #73, "The Lord lift you up"
HWB #433, "Go, my children"

Appendix

Guidelines for writing a mission statement

Writing a mission statement can be a helpful process to clarify purpose and direction in life. Rooted in personal strengths and abilities, tapping into our deepest values and greatest joy that responds to the needs of the world, a mission statement helps us identify and live out our God-given call. A short, concise statement that encompasses all aspects of our lives provides an easy compass point to which we can return again and again as our life circumstances change.

Following are some questions and activities you may find useful in writing your mission statement.

Rooted in personal strengths and abilities

1. What motivates and energizes me? When I feel fulfilled, what am I doing? What do I want or desire most deeply?

2. List the talents, abilities, and interests you possess. Include your accomplishments, volunteer activities, and relational strengths, as well as academic and professional abilities. Come up with at least twenty of these.

3. Identify ten moments in your life where you experienced "flow"—that is, being lost in the experience or activity and feeling fully absorbed and energized.

4. Describe your passion for life in one sentence. What is it that you cannot *not* do?

Summarize your self-knowledge from this process and then boil it down into three action words (for example: create, inspire, express, direct, compose, research).

Tapping into your deepest values and greatest gladness

1. What excites me most in the world? What angers me most? If I taught a class on these issues, what would I want others to know?

2. What events in my life had the most formative impact on who I am today? Who are the people who contributed most to my growth and development? What life circumstances shaped my life direction?

3. What values do I hold most dear? If I had six months to live, what would I be doing? What do I want people to remember about who I am? What legacy do I want to leave?

Based on your lessons from life experiences and relationships, identify six to ten core values you hold. You may want to create a timeline to help in this process. Then rank the values, allowing one core value to rise to the top.

Responding to the needs of the world

1. Identify and prioritize the causes about which you feel passionate. Is there a specific group of people, an entity for which you feel a particular draw?

2. When reflecting on your unique gifts and skills and your particular core value, where does the still small voice of God direct your attention? Toward whom or what is your compassion inspired?

Identify the "needs of the world" to which God is calling you. This can be broad or more specific.

Put the pieces together

Laurie Beth Jones in her book, *The Path*, suggests the following formula for writing a mission statement. It should be one sentence in length, able to be understood by a twelve-year-old, and easily memorized and recited:

Write the statement using three action words, your core value, and for whom your mission is directed:

> My mission is to ______________, __________________,
> and ________________ (*three verbs*) ________________,
> (*core value or values*) *to*, *for* or *with* __________________
> (*group/entity/cause that most resonates*).

Live with the statement for a while, changing words and phrases as needed until you experience inner peace and God's blessing on your mission.

After completing your mission statement, you can develop specific, present-tense, action-oriented vision statements for various aspects of your life and activities. You may have a vision for a particular business, program, family life, fitness plan, or hobby. Vision statements become the actions that carry us forward with our mission in particular areas of life, work, and service.

References:

Jones, Laurie Beth. *The Path: Creating Your Mission Statement for Work and for Life*. New York: Hyperion, 1996.

Palmer, Parker J. *Let your Life Speak: Listening for the Voice of Vocation*. San Francisco: Josey Bass, 2000.

About Mennonite Women Canada

"A Place to Belong"

Motto

As each has received a gift, employ it for one another, as good stewards of God's varied grace. 1 Peter 4:10

Mission statement

Mennonite Women Canada (MW Canada) encourages women to be personally reconciled and committed to Christ and seeks to call forth the variety of gifts given by the Holy Spirit to build the church of Jesus Christ.

We commit ourselves to:

- Promote spiritual growth through Bible study, prayer, other Christian disciplines and fellowship
- Discern and nurture women's gifts and skills for leadership and service in the local church, the community and the world
- Build relationships and networks for support, affirmation, discernment, witness, service and celebration
- Support and strengthen the mission outreach of **Mennonite Church Canada**

We do this through:

- Annual meeting and workshop at Mennonite Church Canada Assembly

- Inter-provincial/regional organizations
- Newsletters
- Scholarships for theological study through **Spiritual Growth Assistance Fund**
- Financial help for young women interested in integrating faith into life through participation in **Radical Journey**, an initiative of Mennonite Church Canada and Mennonite Mission Network
- **Pennies & Prayer Inheritance Fund** (PPIF), a home for gifts made in honour/memory of loved ones
- Supporting women working in Mennonite Church Canada's ministries with funds from the PPIF
- Stories of **"Women Walking Together in Faith"** in ***Canadian Mennonite***
- Publishing an annual Anabaptist Bible study guide with Mennonite Women USA
- A blogspot: www.mennowomencanada.blogspot.com

We as Mennonite Women Canada are striving to do God's will and work where we are to the best of our ability. You too can be a part!

For more information, visit the Mennonite Women Canada website at www.mennonitechurch.ca/mwc/.

Or write to:
Mennonite Women Canada
c/o Mennonite Church Canada
600 Shaftesbury Blvd.
Winnipeg, MB R3P 0M4

About Mennonite Women USA

Jesus said: "I am the vine. You are the branches." John 15:5

Mission statement

Our mission at Mennonite Women USA is to empower women and women's groups as we nurture our life in Christ through studying the Bible, using our gifts, hearing each other, and engaging in mission and service.

In living our mission, Mennonite Women USA:

- Connects globally by funding scholarships for women worldwide for church leadership training through our **International Women's Fund**.

- Equips women for caring ministry through **Sister Care seminars**. Sister Care validates women's gifts of caring and equips them to respond more effectively and confidently to the needs of others in their lives and in the congregation.

- Resources women's groups across the United States through leadership training, an annual Anabaptist Bible study guide, and *timbrel* magazine. Sister Care seminars are hosted by area conference women.

- Speaks prophetically and shares stories of women of all ages and backgrounds through ***timbrel* magazine**, the publication of Mennonite Women USA. *timbrel* is published six times a year and invites women to be "in conversation together with God."

- Fosters relationships around the world through the **Sister-Link program**—emphasizing mutual giving and receiving and validating a wide variety of gifts. Sister-Links connect women through prayer, letter writing, sharing resources, and face-to-face visits.

- Co-sponsors **Women in Conversation retreats** every two years in the East and the Midwest—a time for spiritual nourishment, reflection with God, and warm fellowship with other women.

Vision statement

Mennonite Women USA invites women across generations, cultures, and places to share and honor our stories, care for each other, and express our prophetic voice boldly as we seek to follow Christ.

We'd love to tell you more about our ministry.

Learn more about Mennonite Women USA programs—and get a little lift in your day—by signing up for our free monthly e-letter, "A Postcard & a Prayer." Just send your name, address, and e-mail to office@MennoniteWomenUSA.org.

You may also access our website for our latest news and stories: www.MennoniteWomenUSA.org.

Mennonite Women USA
718 Main St.
Newton, KS 67114-1819
316.281.4396 or 866.866.2872, ext. 34396
office@MennoniteWomenUSA.org

About the Writer

Terri J. Plank Brenneman, PhD, is a clinical psychologist residing in Goshen, Indiana, where she serves as presidential spouse at Goshen College. She holds a doctoral degree from Fuller Theological Seminary in Pasadena, California, as well as a master's in theology and a master's in marriage and family therapy. A graduate of Goshen College, Terri's BA is in social work.

Before moving to Goshen, Terri lived with her husband, Jim Brenneman, son Quinn, and cat, Jazz, in Pasadena. There she maintained a private psychotherapy practice for fifteen years, specializing in adult issues of depression, anxiety, infertility, adult development, and life span consulting. In addition, Terri helped plant Pasadena Mennonite Church, serving in music and worship leadership for twenty years. She and her family now attend Berkey Avenue Mennonite Fellowship in Goshen.

Terri has taught courses in Pastoral Care and Counseling at Fuller Theological Seminary and Associated Mennonite Biblical Seminary and provides coaching sessions to professionals.

Terri has served on the Mennonite Education Agency Board, as president of Pacific Southwest Mennonite Women, president of the bi-national Mennonite Women, and on the former Mennonite Church General Board. She has led women's seminars and retreats in the United States and Canada.

Terri finds great meaning and restoration in silent retreats. For pleasure, she plays piano, gardens, reads, and attends her son's marching band competitions. She enjoys tea and walks with her labradoodle in the woods behind her house.